MARTY STUART
pilgrims

sinners, saints, and prophets

MARTY STUART

pilgrims

sinners, saints, and prophets

a book of words and photographs

Rutledge Hill Press® NASHVILLE, TENNESSEE

Published by Rutledge Hill Press,® Inc., 211 Seventh Avenue North, Nashville, Tennessee 37219-1823.

Distributed in Australia by The Five Mile Press Pty., Ltd., 22 Summit Road, Noble Park, Victoria 3174.
Distributed in Canada by H. B. Fenn & Company, Ltd., 34 Nixon Road, Bolton, Ontario L7E 1W2.
Distributed in New Zealand by Southern Publishers Group, 22 Burleigh Street, Grafton, Auckland.
Distributed in the United Kingdom by Verulam Publishing, Ltd., 152a Park Street Lane, Park Street, St. Albans, Hertfordshire AL2 2AU.

Cover photos by Marty Stuart
Cover design by Schwalb Creative Communications, Inc.
Text design by Schwalb Creative Communications, Inc.
Production by Robert Clay White, Manuscript Ink™, and
    Roger A. DeLiso, Rutledge Hill Press®
Photographs by Marty Stuart

Library of Congress Cataloging-in-Publication Data:
Stuart, Marty.
    Pilgrims : sinners, saints, and prophets : a book of words
        and photographs / Marty Stuart.
        p. cm.
    ISBN 1-55853-773-2
    1. Country musicians—United States Biography.   2. Country
musicians—United States Portraits.   I. Title.
ML394.S88   1999
    781.642'092'273—dc21
        [B]   99-38150
                                                            CIP

Printed in the United States of America
1 2 3 4 5 6 7 8 9—04 03 02 01 00 99

Permissions

To Alfred Steiglitz for taking the photograph of the airplane, Diane Arbus for showing me the edge, and Edward S. Curtis and Karl Moon for allowing me to breathe the dust of their integrity. Thank you, Milt Hinton, for having the foresight to take a camera along on your jazz journey. Les Leverette for your passion in documenting the family of country music. Eudora Welty for giving me a glimpse into my heritage and a very different time in Mississippi. Love to you, my friend Ed Clark, you national treasure, you. You proved that you can get as much soul out of a photograph as Hank Williams did a song. Here's to the heartbeat of the Photo Gallery on Royal Street in New Orleans; long may you live. Thank you, Thomas B. Allen, for inspiring me to view music and photographs as paintings.

The Nashville guys, Bill Thorup and Dan Loftin, for the years of friendship in front of and behind the lens. Thank you, Jim McGuire, for putting the twang back into black and white photography. Ron Keith, you are a genius for breaking every rule in the manual of photography. I thank you for the new rules you've innovated for the other hot shots to break.

Anne Brown, thanks for encouraging me to frame my photographs and hang them on a wall, and for giving me the prestige of calling it an exhibit. To John Folsom and the Chromatics Family in Nashville, thank you for bringing the images to life. To Cathy O'Bryant for your artistry.

Bob Schwalb, thank you for your design of this book. Clay White, your assistance has been invaluable. Willie Wilson, I owe you a new car for all the trips to the warehouse to find negatives. Thanks to Chet Flippo for helping me find Woody's words, and to Nora Guthrie, the Guthrie Family, and the Gene Autry Museum.

To Maria-Elena Orbea (MVP), for taking all my unreadable chicken scratch and translating it into the words of this book, and for bringing order to twenty-five years worth of negatives and contact sheets. Bonnie Garner, thank you for helping me make another dream come true. Thank you, Andy Corn, for taking so much time with me in the early days. I miss you buddy.

Thanks to Margaret Langstaff for beating the streets to get me a deal. And to Larry Stone for giving me a shot and for keeping me humble by reminding me what the true value of my pictures and words are: $29.95 hardback. Less than that when I go on sale.

To Momma

pilgrims

I first went on the road to play music when I was twelve years old. Some parts of America still had dirt floors. You could buy gas for twenty-four cents a gallon, and most every town still owned its own soul. Early on in life, I knew that my calling lay out there somewhere in the world, and from the minute I left home, it became a treasure hunt to find it. All it took to light my fire for the journey was one round of applause. After that, I fell head over heels in love with a thinly veiled disguise better known as the gypsy lifestyle. The road and all its trappings were my utopia—the ultimate parlor of cool. I instantly recognized it as a playground that would kiss you, then kill you. It was a spider web with its own set of rules. And characters . . . there were lots of characters running around.

They're what I loved the most. In those days it was a badge of honor to be an individualist and to bring something original to the table. I never saw a right crowd or a wrong crowd—just people on a journey in search of whatever their mission was. Some were on their way up and riding high. Some were coming down and barely surviving. I saw the best and the worst of intentions. There were wannabees, should've beens, could've beens, has beens, musicians, poets, songwriters, singers, drivers, janitors, doormen, executives, waitresses, gospel singers, dead ringers, horse traders, carnies, drunks, misfits, spies, dancers, jugglers, fans, groupies, sharks, clowns, smugglers, song pluggers, mechanics, pushers, preachers, hobos, addicts, and various other snooking agents of all sorts. I was fascinated by the whole show. I saw it as one big eccentric family and I wanted to find my place to fit in.

My situation and its surroundings were unique. After graduating from my summer starter course on the backroads circuit with the Sullivan Family, I toured the nation with Lester Flatt's band. Lester and his wife, Gladys, took me into their home to live with them shortly after I came to Nashville, until my family could make arrangements to follow.

I was three years away from being old enough to drive, so wherever Lester went, so did I. His peers became my pals. All of a sudden, Ernest Tubb, Roy Acuff, Bill Monroe, Grandpa Jones, and Stringbean were a big part of my life. I had total access to the wit and wisdom of some of the greatest architects of American music. Whether it was to have lunch or to go fishing, when any of these guys got together, I viewed it as a historic occasion.

One day, one of the veterans in Lester's band made the comment, "I'd give anything if I'd had a camera and a tape recorder when we played that show with Elvis and the rest of them. Think of what I'd have now." I took his statement to heart. I asked Momma for a camera, and she gave me a Kodak Instamatic for Christmas. I carried it along with me and proceeded to terrorize anybody that had ever sang, written, or played a country song. It was no more than a hobby to me. I simply took snapshots that went along with the stories that followed me home from the road.

The main person that I shared my hobby with was Momma. Although she was never formally trained, she always shot great photos. Her pictures have a dignified yet informal quality about them that I admire. She sees the treasures. Her shots ring true because she shoots from the heart. If I have anything that

(Photo by George Day)

resembles a photographer's style, it would be the style I took from her—sort of an "I'm the only one at the family reunion who thought to bring a camera" style. I don't care much for staged photographs; I love the unguarded side of people because it shows the essence of their souls.

Most everyone in this book has a specific call on their lives, and they've sacrificed a great deal for it. They affect numerous people in various ways. Whether it's Brother Phillip Holloway pounding the backroads of Louisiana to spread the Gospel of Christ, or Brother Keith Richards pounding the universe with his guitar to spread the message of rock & roll, they're all pilgrims. They are the special people who answer to the jangle in their souls while they touch us with the magic that God gave them.

By now, I truly thought I'd have running the roads out of my blood. But I'm beginning to wonder if there's really an end in sight for me. That line that Merle Haggard wrote hits a little too close for comfort when I hear it now. "I want to die along the highway and rot away like some old high-line pole. Then I'll rest this rambling fever in my soul." In the end, it's the soul that matters. Fame dies, glory fades, and when the line is drawn, we will all have to stand accountable for which side we were on and how we handled our journey . . . like sinners, saints, or prophets.

I am a lonesome pilgrim
far from home,
and what a journey
I have known.
I might be tired and weary,
but I am strong,
'cause pilgrims walk,
but not alone.

—Marty Stuart

The sign reads:

I PUSHED MYSELF UP
HILL - 24 - YEARS FOR
YOU TO COAST DOWN
IN ONE DAYS. VISIT MY
CONTRIBUTION TO ALL
MANKIND. ANIMALS AND BIRDS
12-31-06-7-20-1985 BY HOWARD FINSTER FROM GOD. 4000-850 WORKS

The extremely cool words *of Howard Finster, Paradise Gardens, Georgia, 1995*

Grandpa Elry *Lee Johnson*

It all goes back to Route 8, Philadelphia, Mississippi. Maybe it was a whippoorwill, maybe it was the smell of magnolia, or maybe it was the sound of a train. Perhaps it was the water in the well or the kick of my grandpa's shotgun against my shoulder. It could've been the first fish I ever caught or when I heard the church bells ring. It might have been the sound of a fiddle, a falling star, a soldier on the courthouse lawn, or the ghost of Mississippi. It might've been the Choctaw Indian at Lake Tiakahata, or when Daddy got that job at the factory, or when I first heard "High Heel Sneakers" or "The Old Rugged Cross." It could've hit me when my sister held onto my arm because she was frightened to have her picture made.

Elry and Alton Adcock *goin' fishin'*

Perhaps it was Porter Wagoner or the Apostle Paul's Damascus Road experience. It might have even been the report of my Uncle Charles Duett getting killed in a late-night scuffle in a Mississippi jailhouse or the cats with gold teeth playing the jukebox loud at the Busy Bee Cafe on Church Street.

Perhaps it was the one-legged man that sold peanuts on the edge of town. It could have been Momma's love, Red Skelton, Sunday school, or a mayonnaise sandwich at Butch Hodgins' house, my wagon, watching my Grandpa Johnson roll a Prince Albert cigarette while surveying the cottonfields from a red dirt road, a Farmahl tractor, my original guitar, a

The Busy Bee Cafe, *Church Street, Philadelphia, Mississippi*

Levi Stuart *and Wilford Barrett, Philadelphia, Mississippi, 1977*

mongoose cage, a birdtrap, finding a hidden whiskey bottle under some pine straw, *The Sound of Music*, the Cub Scouts, my kindergarten diploma, *Dennis the Menace*, a postcard from Washington, D.C., boiled peanuts, a summer rain, our maid, Jimmie Richmond's tears on the ironing board when she heard that Otis Redding had died, a pair of cowboy boots, Momma's fried chicken, standing on the hood of Daddy's truck and holding onto my sister while we watched Dr. Martin Luther King Jr. march through our town, or Aunt Pinky Darby playing sour notes on the piano at Old Pearl Valley Baptist Church as we all cried and told

Grandpa Levi *Lincoln Stuart*

Pa *and his hound*

My first *bus*

Wilson
Melton

my Grandma Stuart good-bye, when Uncle Rudolph gave me his
Johnny Cash record, or just sitting in the yard under the wheel of
his car and pretending I knew how to drive and was on my way to
somewhere, peeing off the back porch, hearing the Pentecostal
people shout and sing, listening to the politicians' speeches at the
Neshoba County Fair, getting baptized, seeing my first country
music star bus come through town, the chlorine in the swimming
pool at the Colonial House Motel, breaking the picture window with
a softball, when that suitcase hit me in the head, when Momma
would drive Sis and I around town during Christmas so we could
see all the pretty lights, the airwaves of WHOC, being a lousy base-
ball player, pulpwood trucks, a clock left over from the Civil War,
when we moved from Choctaw Gardens to Koskiusko Road, my job
as a greeting card salesman, revival at our church, the water in the
spring, new tomatoes, when Welch Moore named me Doc, Lacy
Crow's services to the community as a volunteer fireman, the time I
got my picture put in the *Neshoba Democrat,* the first time I sang a
song in public, got stitches, the day I noticed Flatt & Scruggs' old
tour bus sitting in Marzell Page's front yard, the Pearl River Swamp,
a Confederate flag, cutting the yard, the autographed picture sent to
me from Eb on *Green Acres,* tonsillitis, when Dick Perry died in a
plane crash, the calendar on the wall with a picture of Daddy on it
when he was a deputy sheriff, my sister winning a hairdryer, my
first cup of coffee, when that catfish finned me, the seventy-five
cents I spent at Frank Tank's discount store on Highway 16E for a

The day Ernest Tubb *came to town*

Sis and I *at the Neshoba County Fair, singing "I've Got a Tiger by the Tail," live over WHOC (photo by Hilda Stuart)*

scratched up 78 rpm record of Bill Monroe and the Bluegrass Quartet's song "Little Community Church," chasing the mosquito truck, Pippa Perry, the air conditioner in Daddy's 1967 Volkswagen, when Pa Johnson left the farm and moved to the Gulf Coast, Hurricane Camille, the *Joby Martin Show*, the Todd Sisters, Gail Dunnigan, when black and white went color, when hi-fi went stereo, the furniture in the lobby of the Benwalt Hotel, when I went to Alabama with Daddy and John Cook to hear Bill Monroe and the Sullivan Family.

Maybe it was the day Connie Smith came to town or that security guard that made me go back to my seat when I was trying to get a closer look at Johnny Cash playing the Coliseum in Jackson. The day President Kennedy died, the day Dr. Martin Luther King Jr. died, the day George Wallace was shot, the day my Daddy was shot, the day the Grand Ole Opry stars died in a plane crash, staring out Ma Stuart's kitchen window and listening to the radio play Patsy Cline songs over and over again all day. Maybe it was the dipper in the water bucket on the

Pa Stuart's *house*

Pa Stuart's *back porch dipper*

back porch, or the pines whispering just enough breeze across Pa Stuart's front porch to move the rocking chairs back and forth with nobody in them. As much as it could have been any of these, it was the Holy Spirit that set down on me and gave me the vision of taking all of those imaginary concerts I played on that porch out of the front yard and into the world. That porch was my theater of dreams. It was there that a feeling came over me that was more than a dream. It was a call on my life. I felt a power well up inside me that made me want to step off that porch and go to the bottom of the driveway, walk up the dirt road to Highway 19, turn left, and start walking toward Koskiusko, then Vaiden, Senatobia, Clarksdale, Oxford, Grenada, straight on into Memphis, and finally Nashville. That's where I felt the music coming from. All these things are like flashcard memories at the core of my soul. They make up the first eleven years of my life. I know them as heartfelt meditations I fall back on when I lose track of myself and need to go home.

Home

July 24, 1970, was a big day for my family. Momma's favorite singer, Connie Smith, was booked to come to our town and sing at the Choctaw Indian Fair. One of the albums that we had of Connie's was "Miss Smith Goes to Nashville." I stared at her picture on that album cover so much that I memorized every detail about her. I thought she was the prettiest girl I'd ever seen. She looked like an angel.

The day of her concert I had Momma take me into town to Seward's Department Store. I picked out a yellow shirt to wear to the fair, hoping it would make me stand out in the crowd enough for Connie Smith to notice me.

After the show, my sister and I got our picture made with Connie. I talked to her musicians, watched her sign autographs for the fans, and waited for her to notice me. She never did. In a last-ditch attempt for recognition, I borrowed my momma's camera and went to the car where Connie was sitting to ask if I could take her picture. She said yes. As it turns out, it was the first photograph I'd ever taken. On the way home I told momma I was going to marry that girl. I did—on July 8, 1997.

My first job on the circuit was playing the mandolin with a group from St. Stephens, Alabama, called the Sullivan Family Gospel Singers. They are well-loved bluegrass musicians, who over the years have carved out a loyal following at Holiness churches, camp meetings, and bluegrass festivals throughout the remnants of the Old South. The Sullivan Family's core audience are spirit-filled, soul-stirring type people—precious people with lots of heart.

Out of all the characters I've ever met, Uncle Emmett Sullivan is still, hands down, the most lovable whacked-out coon dog I've ever traveled with. He taught me the importance of having as much fun on the road as you can without dying and the essence of treating show business with every ounce of irreverence it deserves. I'll always be grateful to him for helping me through my first case of homesick blues. I was on the verge of tears. He told me the best way to get over being homesick on the road was to hoodoo a monkey.

Camp meeting, *Emmett, Enoch, and Sister Margie, 1972*

The Sullivan Family

How to *hoodoo a monkey*

As *Mr. Allen*

As *Lamb Chops Areno*

Taking *the good folks' money*

I didn't have a clue what he was talking about, so he said he'd teach me.

A few miles down the road, we stopped at a Dixie Service Station that was one of those combination filling stations and fireworks stands. Their drawing cards were cheap gas and a monkey that chain-smoked cigarettes in a cage over by the drink machines. When we got out of the car, Emmett told me to follow him. He lit a cigarette and gave it to the monkey. Just as the monkey began his puffing act, Emmett started speaking in a language known only to the two of them. The monkey threw down the cigarette and started screaming and running around in circles. Uncle Emmett moved in closer and dead-eyed him. Then he dropped his dentures down so that he favored a gorilla and hypnotized that monkey into a stone-cold trance.

That night we played a church and two people got saved. I remember thinking, this is how absurd the road could be. One minute, you're hoodooing a monkey, and the next, you're trying to lead somebody to the Lord.

Sunset at Bean Blossom

Lester Flatt, *Berkshire Mountain Bluegrass Festival, 1977*

I saw Lester Flatt in person for the first time at Bill Monroe's Bean Blossom Bluegrass Festival in 1971. I looked at the program and found out what time he was playing, and I stood by his bus to watch him come out. When he did, the speech I'd planned kind of got lost inside me. About the only thing I managed to say was, "Hello."

It was close to a quarter of a mile of dirt road from the parking lot to the stage at Bean Blossom. I followed him the entire way. I studied him. I loved the way he cocked his hat. He had on a black suit with a white shirt and a red tie, and he was wearing the first patent leather shoes I'd ever seen. He walked very slowly through the dust and the sea of campers. People sort of changed as he passed, like the effect of a preacher walking through a poker game. Musicians, hippies, bikers, old folks, and kids all wanted to just touch him.

Douglas, Georgia

Bill Monroe

Lester Flatt

Lester Flatt, *Douglas, Georgia*

My Nashville career began Labor Day weekend 1972. I was expelled from school after I got caught reading *Country Song Roundup* magazine in history class. I got so involved in the magazine that I lost track of my teacher. She slipped up behind me and grabbed my book. She told me if I'd get my mind off that trash and get it onto history that I might make something of myself. I told her I was more interested in making history than reading about it. She sent me and my smart mouth to the principal's office. I passed his office without stopping and kept right on walking. I walked home and called a friend of mine, named Roland White, who worked with Lester. I'd met Roland earlier in the year at a bluegrass festival, and he'd made a casual remark which I had straight away put in my pocket. He said, "Maybe some weekend, if it's all right with your folks, I'll ask Lester if you can go along with us for a trip." School had barely started. After a summer of being free as a bird and playing music, getting thrown back into a world where names like Bill Monroe and Flatt & Scruggs were virtually nonexistent was not exactly the kind of

Boardroom meeting, *Higgin's Gulf Station, Hendersonville, Tennessee*

life I was looking for anymore. I was a pretty sorry excuse for a student. At the time, I felt I did myself and the Philadelphia High School a great service by leaving.

I had to beg my folks to let me go, but they finally gave in and agreed to let me travel for the weekend. However, deep in my heart I knew that I wouldn't be coming back for a while.

That weekend turned into a career. Lester and I hit it off immediately. He heard Roland and me fooling around on the mandolin and the guitar in the back of the bus. He kind of laughed and said, "Why don't you do that on the show this weekend?" At the end of the weekend he offered me a job.

The *office*

After a good deal of negotiation with my folks, it was agreed that I would spend the next portion of my life in a tired old Greyhound scenic cruiser that had been converted into a submarine clubhouse atmosphere and was home to Lester Flatt and the Nashville Grass. It was kind of like joining the Navy. My formal training ground would be a sea of the finest concert halls, studios, and cow pastures in the nation. (photo by Hilda Stuart, Heber Springs, Arkansas, 1972)

I walked past Lester's room on the bus one afternoon and this is what I saw. It made me cry. I felt really sleazy when I took the picture, because I knew I was intruding into his innermost privacy. The reason I took the picture was so I could remember what a precious old road warrior he was. The photograph is entitled "Dedication," because he had no other reason to be on the road for the last couple of years of his life. His health was so poor that he had to sit down on stage, be attended by a nurse, and rely on oxygen to help him breathe. But he fought it to the very end. It was incredible to witness the relationship between Lester and his fans. Some nights after he was introduced, we couldn't play because of all the cheering and the applause. He'd have to wait five minutes for the crowd to settle down. Then he'd give it all he had.

Dedication

"Long Journey Home,"
Lester's final tour, fall 1978

Bill Monroe, *Jackson, Kentucky*

Bluegrass

Grandpa *Jones*

"The people that play this kind of music know about the ancient tones."
—*Bill Monroe*

Roy *Acuff*

"King" *Jimmy Martin*

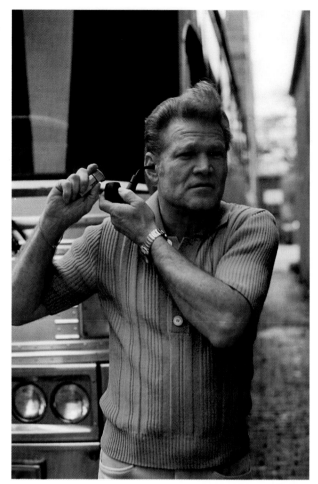

Vassar Clements *in St. Louis*

Pete *and Tex*

Sonny Osborne, *the chairman of cool*

Snuffy *Jenkins*

Clinch Mountain Boys, *Ralph Stanley*
and Curly Ray Cline

Kenny *Baker*

Dutton

Hope *Randolph*

Greasy Medlin
the Clown

The Blue *Goose*

Bob Dylan is one of the most magical human beings I've ever met. He's like the pied piper. When he leaves a room, people follow him without knowing where he's leading them. One of my favorite pastimes is "Bob watching." I love watching him do his song and dance on the world. He's one cool move after another.

I never know when I'm going to run into Bob Dylan. It's never planned. The first time was in the 1970s. He came to Nashville to do a concert. I was hanging around in the lobby of the hotel, talking to some musicians. He came over and said, "Aren't you the kid that plays the mandolin or something?"

I was five years old the first time I heard Johnny Cash's voice. It crept into my heart and has lived there ever since. I had three records then. *Meet the Beatles, Flatt & Scruggs Greatest Hits,* and *The Fabulous Johnny Cash.* I gave the Beatles record away and kept the other two.

What drew me into him was the fact he wasn't your ordinary hillbilly singer. He was dark. He sounded to me as though he was singing from a room that had seen better days, with only one light bulb hanging down from the ceiling. I felt like too much light shining on him made him uncomfortable. I saw him as a shadow on the wall—a mystery—regal as they come, yet common as a biscuit. I had the feeling that if I were to run with him, I'd see my share of trouble. But I didn't care. It'd be worth it.

Since the day I set my eyes on him back then, I've never let him out of my sight. I watch every move he makes. Even when I was

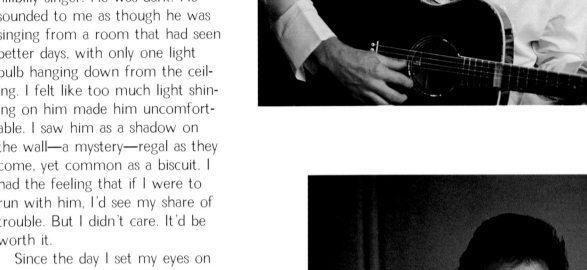

The day *I met him*

Two Great *Americans*

John *with John Carter Cash*

Johnny and June *on the road*

a kid, I knew I'd meet him. I believe God sometimes lays people on your heart early on, just so you can prepare to know them later. I met him in 1979. When we shook hands I heard thunder. It changed my life. He means something to everybody. He has a great gift of touching people's hearts. All walks of life claim him. He's one of the greatest interpreters of human emotion that's ever been. He's a lot of different characters wrapped up inside of one man. The world knows him as Johnny Cash. The cats call him Johnny. June calls him John. His mama and daddy called him J. R.

Today, we're blood close. But there was another time when we were even closer. Starting in the early 1980s, I played in his band for six years. I was around him all the time. During this period, I had a microscopic view of his world. It was a big ride that forged its way across the Earth with the grace of

"Daddy sang bass, *Momma sang tenor"*

a rabid cyclone. Following him around was an amazing adventure. He is without a doubt the most charismatic man God ever made. Watching him peel an apple is just as interesting as seeing him perform on stage. His charisma is hard to put into words, but it's something that the camera understands.

When I first went to work with him, he was deep into photography. He usually carried with him a black Haliburton-type case full of cameras and lenses. Watching him take pictures inspired me to bring my camera out of a three-year slump and start shooting again. It put me back into the frame of mind that made me pay attention to the details of what was going on around me. And even on the most normal of days, behind the

scenes in John and June's world, it's a pretty fascinating show. There's always something interesting going on.

I saw everything from a prisoner's mother get down on her hands and knees in front of J. R. and beg him to help her get her son off Death Row to a little boy who came backstage to ask him to pull his tooth. It was a special time. Like the line in the song says, "you can check out anytime, but you can never leave." Once you're a part of him, he's always a part of you. It's a lifetime deal.

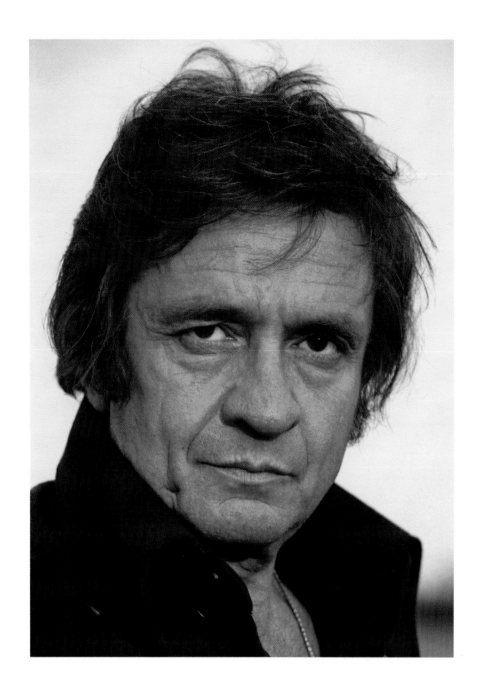

Cash *and the Cowboy*

Psychobilly *Cowboy*

The president *of the United States, Washington, D.C.*

Hard times *and misery*

Under bridges,
beneath trestles,
in the boxcars of
dead trains,
living to beat the cold
of the pouring, driving rain,
a silent society moves out
in the night,
ragged rebels, homeless hobos, and those like me
who've lost the light.

St. Peter is a prophet to all the hobo world,
an expert on everything from caviar to girls.
I met him west of Memphis on the 8th of July.
He handed me a can of beans and a rusty knife,

and he said, "Everything out here
ain't what it seems.
When you're down
to nothing,
just go ahead and dream.
Face the fact that
you're a circle
in a world full of squares,
trading sorrows for
tomorrows.
That's the hobo's prayer."

St. Peter,
the trainyard prophet,
West Memphis, Arkansas

Wrongway Skidmark,
Tupelo, Mississippi

I met Ethan Allen one afternoon while I was taking a walk around New Port Richey, Florida. John and June had a concert booked in town and the band had arrived a couple of days early to relax and enjoy some time around one of the Cashs' summer homes.

Ethan Allen lived in a tiny trailer that was hidden in a palm grove close to the Cashs' house. When I first saw him, I was intrigued by his appearance. I introduced myself and told him that I admired his hat. He said, "Well you should. George Washington gave it to me. I wouldn't take a million dollars for it, so don't try to buy it." He added that people had come from all over the world just to look at it. He finally got tired of the attention and that, he said, was why he'd gone into seclusion. I told him I fully understood. He asked me what type of work I was in, and I told him I was a guitar player in a rockabilly band. He said, "I'm an entertainer myself. I'm a man of the theater. I have pictures and reviews to prove it." And he did. He went inside his trailer and brought out a cigar box full of memories that he shared with me. I remarked that he looked familiar. He said, "Of course I do."

When it was time to go, I asked him if I could take his photograph. He said he had only two conditions: (1) people usually paid him five dollars for the privilege, and (2) they had to take their photographs with black and white film. I apologized and told him that I only used color film. He said, "You're making a great mistake. The truth is hidden in black and white. You'll see things differently if you listen to me." I asked him if I came back with black and white film that afternoon could I take the shot. He said, "You know the terms."

I found a camera shop and bought some black and white film. I went back, gave him five dollars, and took his picture. When he pulled out his wallet to park my five, he said, "Let me show you the power of a black and white photograph." He showed me a small portrait of himself on an old ID badge from Hughes Aviation. The name read HOWARD HUGHES—FULL ACCESS. I told him that I began to see what he meant about the truth being hidden somewhere between black and white.

When I started to leave, he said, "Yes sir, I've been offered a million dollars for this hat."

I said, "I've only got twenty-five dollars on me today."

He said, "Well, since it's you, I'll take it."

When I developed the film, I saw things in a different light. All of a sudden everything looked more real in black and white. So, thank you, Ethan Allen, whoever you are.

Ethan Allen,
New Port Richey,
Florida, early 1980s

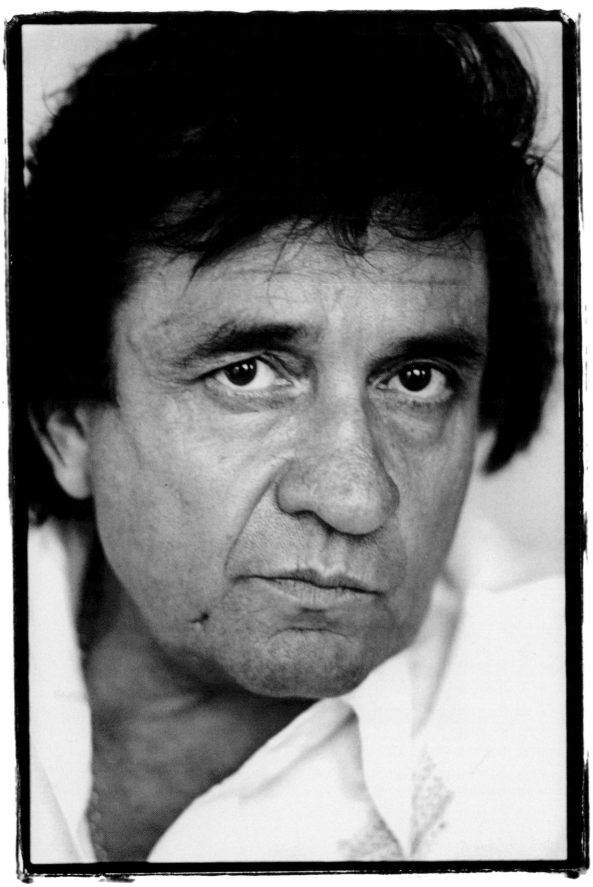

John R. *Cash*

On the road *in Minnesota*

Touchin' *the folks*

I had finally saved up enough money to buy a good mandolin after I went to work for Lester Flatt. It cost $650 and it was the only instrument I've ever owned that I took pride in. When I went to work for Johnny Cash, my mandolin didn't have a scratch on it.

J. R. got on a kick of playing it. It worked out good, because I got a kick out of watching him. One night on stage, he stopped playing in mid-song, took out his pocketknife, and began to carve his initials on the front of my mandolin. Then he scratched his name on the back. For a big finish, he carved a big cross on the top.

After the show, I asked him why he did it. He said he wanted me to remember the Lord. I told him I could have remembered the Lord without him wrecking my mandolin. But I really didn't care. Now my mandolin is full of names. I've never asked for many of the signatures. People just felt obligated to sign it.

Salem

Ohio

The Survivors
Carl Perkins, Jerry Lee Lewis, Johnny Cash
Hamburg, Germany

Memphis is a powerful, mystical city. In Memphis you can be lifted to the foot of the cross or stand close enough to the devil to smell his breath. It has to be approached with extreme caution or it will slide right out from under you. These three kings were trained in Memphis and could testify to that. A living testimony that they'd been to hell and back and lived to tell it was a package tour across Europe in 1982 billed as "The Survivors." The rockabilly fans ate it up. It was greased lightning.

powerful

survivors

mystical

Jerry Lee Lewis, *Johnny Cash, Carl Perkins*

The Survivors *in Germany*

Me and Uncle Gerald,
Sun Studio, Memphis, Tennessee

For two days in 1983, starting backstage at a concert in Paris, I tried to keep up with "The Killer." I remember . . .

. . . seeing Jerry Lee hold a promoter at gunpoint, while he prayed for him to remember what happened to the rest of the money at the box office.

. . . French girls.

. . . standing in an open-roof Mercedes Benz limousine and singing Hank Williams songs as we cruised the Champs Elysees.

. . . more French girls.

. . . answering a knock on my hotel-room door around 4 a.m. and finding Jerry Lee outside, covered from head to toe with chocolate cake, asking if he could borrow my fiddle. I haven't seen it since.

. . . hearing Jerry Lee preach some incredibly prophetic, hellfire sermonettes, denouncing rock & roll and everything associated with it. Then witnessing this master showman walk on stage and deliver one of the greatest tent-revival, Louisiana Barrell House, boogaloo shows of the century.

By the end, I had come to understand that when God made Jerry Lee Lewis, He had truly made a special person. Jerry Lee is one of the most natural musical geniuses of our time. Somewhere along the way, he became my favorite eccentric uncle.

Rocking

my life away

*Nuremberg,
Germany*

"You cannot go to heaven and play rock & roll"

Whole lot of

Rockabillys, *Paris, France*

shaking

"The Killer"

Moetta

Paris

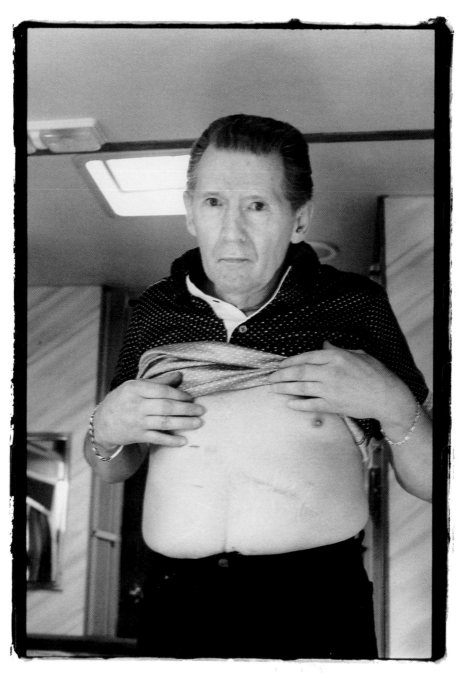

1996

"**The Archangel** *of Rock & Roll"*

One of the true highlights of my life was a week in the summer of 1985 when producer Chips Moman put together a project called the Class of '55 Reunion. Johnny Cash, Jerry Lee Lewis, Carl Perkins, and Roy Orbison returned to Memphis to record and film the sessions at Sun Studio and American Sound. Journalists came from all over the world to cover it. Rockabillies, such as Rick Nelson, John Fogerty, and Dave Edmunds, and their keepers came to enjoy the music and feed on the spirit. I was there as a Cash band member and session player. Roy Orbison delivered the most heartfelt moment of the week when he sang "I'm Coming Home." Ten years after the sessions I found a roll of film marked "Memphis '85." I had no idea what was on it. When I had it developed, only three frames were exposed. Right before we had recorded "I'm Coming Home," I snapped this shot.

Rocket *Fuel,*

Hairspray,

and the same old town one more time

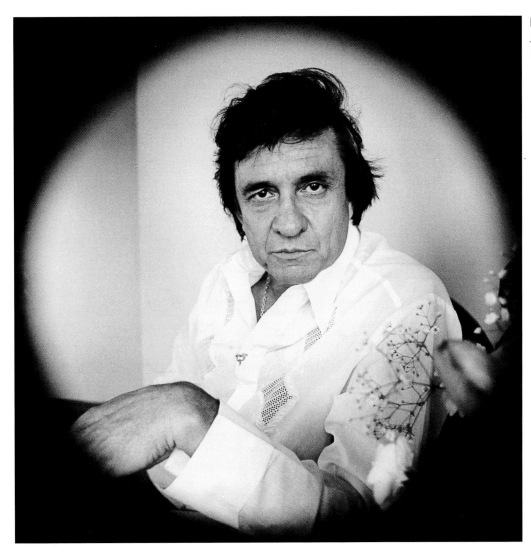

Johnny Cash's
2 A.M. tribute to John Lennon, Australia, early 1980s

'll try and carry off a little darkness on my back, till things are brighter. I'm the Man in Black.

—*Johnny Cash*

Two members of the elite sorority, *SWWRASFTK (Southern Women Who Received a Scarf from the King), Memphis, Tennessee, early 1980s*

Before *Graceland became a star*

Jessi's
Party

1985

Jessi Colter threw one of the best parties Nashville has ever seen. The theme was the 50s. The celebration was in honor of Waylon Jennings and Johnny Cash's new found sobriety. We all hid our dope and went. Willie, Robert Duvall, Hank Jr., and limos full of other celebrities came by to congratulate Johnny and Waylon for being strong.

Willie *and Waylon*

People *at a party*

Earl "Poole" Ball *and acquaintances*

We went to Montreux, Switzer

Country Music's *Mount Rushmore, 1985*

We went to Montreux, Switzerland, to film a Johnny Cash Christmas Special in 1984. The guests were Waylon Jennings, Willie Nelson, and Kris Kristofferson. At the end of the day, after the filming on location was completed, everyone gathered in John and June's suite to sing songs, swap stories, and pass the guitar around. The four were all close friends except John and

Willie, who really didn't know each other that well. But after they finally had more than twenty minutes together, they formed a friendship. At the end of it all, they agreed to get together and record a duet album as soon as their tours let up.

When we got home, Chips Moman set up the sessions. He didn't know exactly what he was looking for. He was just riding on the feelings from

Montreux. After a day or two in the studio, we still hadn't accomplished much, so I did the only thing I knew to do—I went out song shopping. I heard about a song Glen Campbell had recorded called "The Highwayman." My cousin ran Glen Campbell's publishing company, and he played me the song. It was incredible. It had four verses. I thought: John, Willie, Kris, Waylon.

I played the song for Chips and John. They dug it. Glen Campbell came by the studio to put down a scratch vocal. Waylon already knew the song, because he'd recorded it on a previous record. John, Willie, and Kris came around one part at a time and the song came to life. The duet became a quartet, the quartet became *The Highwaymen*.

J. R. signing *Willie's guitar*

Connie and Willie Nelson, *Montreux, Switzerland*

Willie Nelson, *Los Angeles, California*

Waymore *working them lines*

Nashville, Tennessee

1985

Waylon

Willie, *Universal Amphitheater, Los Angeles, California*

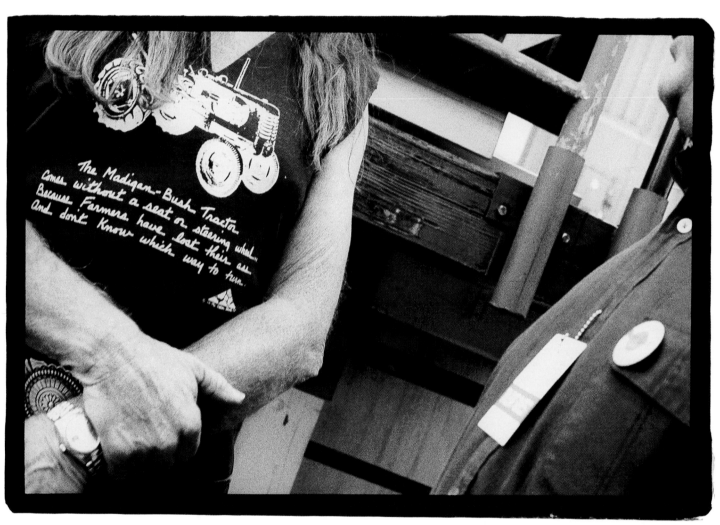

The Madigan-Bush Tractor Comes without a seat or steering wheel... Because Farmers have lost their ass and don't know which way to turn.

Willie *Nelson's shirt*

The first time I went to California was in 1974. For months I'd saved my money to go to Nudie's Western Store. I had $250 burning a hole in my checkbook. The band dropped me off to shop while they went to a restaurant. When I walked into that store it was like walking into a sparkle factory. I was totally overwhelmed.

Nudie said, "Can I help you?"

I said, "Yes sir. I'm here to buy a rhinestone suit."

I picked one off the rack and fell in love with it. When I asked how much it was, Nudie said $2500. It broke my heart. It devastated me.

Manuel was the head tailor at Nudie's then, and he saw the disappointment in my face. He said, "Kid, what is your name?" and I told him.

He said, "My name is Manuel. Some day you'll come in here and buy lots of suits. Today, you get a free shirt." He pulled an embroidered cowboy shirt off the rack and gave it to me. I still have it. It's one of my most cherished gifts.

Manuel's act of kindness that day started a bond of friendship and brotherhood that exists to this very minute. Since then, he's become my big brother, advisor, confidante, image consultant, favorite honky tonkin' compadre, critic, educator on mariachi bands, and philosopher. I've lost count of all the clothes he's made for me. Every single outfit stands on its own as a work of art. However, there's one that means more to me than any of the rest.

In the mid-1980s, when I was going through some rocky times and running wild in the streets, he tracked me down at a bar in Nashville. I don't know how he found me, but when he got me on the phone, he said, "I hear you're messing up and ruining

Manuel, *1999*

your reputation. What's the matter with you? You know better. I want you to get on an airplane and come see me, so we can talk this out face to face."

I said, "I don't have any money."

He said, "Your ticket is at the counter and I'll have you picked up at the airport."

I flew to Los Angeles and stayed with him for a few days. During my stay there, he made me spill my guts. The main thing I discovered about myself was how sad I was. I had completely lost my self-esteem. I had a terrible self-image and I felt defeated.

The last day I was there, I noticed he had called in some extra workers. They worked around the clock on a beautiful black leather suit that had custom hand-engraved sterling silver conchos all over it. It was a masterpiece. As I was saying good-bye, he said, "Do me a favor; try this suit on. I want to see how it looks."

I tried it on and joked, "It's great, but it's too big in the chest and the shoulders are too broad."

He said, "Not if you stand up straight and stick out your chest. It's time for you to be a man." He gave it to me. I knew it was his way of saying, "I believe in you." As long as I've known him, I've never seen him put that much of himself into a suit of clothes. He'll never know how much that meant to me. It was the only new cowboy suit I had for a long time. When I finally got my recording contract and some work to go with it, I wore that suit on all of my first appearances.

To this day, when I'm troubled, I go to his store and either sit or lay down on his cutting room table and watch him while he creates. For some strange reason it gives me peace.

Pa Stuart, *Philadelphia, Mississippi, early 1980s*

The day *Daddy retired, 1995*

Sis's Birthday and Momma's *retirement party,*
Rio Bravo Cantina, Nashville, Tennessee, 1996

Aunt Lou Don Gamblin,
Van Cleave, Mississippi

A Day in Poor Valley,

There are places out there in the world which I refer to as invisible filling stations where I go to rekindle myself. One of those places I find myself returning to time and time again when the road takes its toll on me is a little town called Hiltons that's nearly in Tennessee and barely in Virginia. Just down the road from Hiltons is Poor Valley, the home of the original Carter Family. Today, A. P. and Sara's children, Joe and Janette, still call it home. Janette has a music barn there called the Carter Fold, and most every Saturday night you'll find her and Joe, along with various other old-time music enthusiasts, playing and preserving the purest form of country music.

Janette and Joe "Bull" Carter, *guardian angels, 1997*

A. P. Carter's *Clinch Mountain home*

Virginia

A. P. Carter (signature)

It's light years away from the commodity that country music has become. The Poor Valley experience is a glimpse into the Appalachian way of life and an opportunity to touch one of the cornerstones of country music's life stream. A trip there is similar to going to a mountain church revival. By the time I've played music with Joe, been fed and loved on by Janette and all the relatives, visited A. P.'s childhood home, picked apple blossoms off his trees, taken flowers to his and Sara's graves, drank water from Maybelle's well, and let the dew from Clinch Mountain settle on my mind, I've usually regained my fire and I'm ready to take on the world again. It's evident to me why God chose Poor Valley, Virginia, as the birthplace of something so special. That was a long time ago, and the feeling is still there. All you have to do is show up—it'll find you.

"The Keeper of the Fold," _Janette Carter's daughter, Rita Forrester, Poor Valley, Virginia, 1997_

"Keep on the Sunny Side," *Hiltons, Virginia, 1997*

I hate a song that makes you think that you are not a good person. I hate a song that makes you think you are just born to lose. Bound to lose. No good to nobody. No good for nothing. Because you are too old or too young or too fat or too slim or too ugly or too this or too that. Songs that run you down or poke fun at you on account of your bad luck or hard traveling.

I am out to fight those songs to my very last breath of air and my last drop of blood. I am out to sing songs that will prove to you that this is your world and that if it has hit you pretty hard and knocked you for a dozen loops, no matter what color, what size you are, how you are built, I am out to sing the songs that make you take pride in yourself and in your work. And the songs that I sing are made up for the best part by all sorts of folks just about like you.

I could hire out to the other side, the big money side, and get several dollars every week just to quit singing my own kind of songs and to sing the kind that knock you down still farther and the ones that poke fun at you even more and the ones that make you think you've not got any sense at all. But I decided a long time ago that I'd starve to death before I'd sing any such songs as that. The radio waves and your movies and your jukeboxes and your songbooks are already loaded down and running over with such no good songs as that anyhow.

—Woody Guthrie

Woody Guthrie's *fiddle, 1999*

THE ODYSSEY OF HARLAN HOWARD
(Be Careful Who You Love)

The old guitar picker had run out of liquor
So I sat down beside him and bought him a drink
I bought him another and finally some color
Returned to his cheeks, and he said with a wink
Son, I worked for Red Foley, knew Hank and Old Lefty
I worked on the Opry back when it was strong
But in showbiz you know, sometimes it gets slow
So buy us another and I'll sing you a song
Be careful who you love, for love can be untrue
Be careful who you love, be sure she loves you too . . .

Buried deep in a publishing catalog alongside such songs as "I Fall To Pieces," "Pick Me Up on Your Way Down," "Life Turned Her That Way," "Heartaches by the Number," "I've Got a Tiger by the Tail," "Too Many Rivers," "Busted," "Why Not Me," "Above and Beyond," "Don't Tell Me What To Do," and "Blame It on Your Heart," there's another Harlan Howard song entitled "Arthur's Song." It's never been a hit. It's not a song that immediately comes to mind when you think of Harlan's body of work. It's a song that was lovingly written and dedicated to an old country songwriter named Arthur Q. Smith.

Arthur lived around Knoxville, Tennessee, and became famous for writing the classic country songs, "Wedding Bells Are Ringing in the Chapel," "I Overlooked an Orchid While Searching for a Rose," "Rainbow at Midnight," and, with near positive proof, "I Can't Stop Loving You." He would sell them to publishers and hot radio singers for whiskey money. His era was the 1940s and early 1950s, but time has left his memory in the distance. Even though they bear other's names, these songs serve as a reminder that he did in fact walk among us.

By no means was this the story of every songwriter. But in the social hierarchy of the music industry in the early years, the songwriter was often seen as a secondary citizen. On September 24, 1997, I witnessed Harlan Howard, the undisputed king of Nashville songwriters, get inducted into the Country Music Hall of Fame. That was the day the status of the country music songwriter was forever lifted and sealed.

The next morning, I ran into Harlan, still celebrating at a local watering hole. He was holding court with some songwriting buddies—"back in the trenches," as he put it. A young songwriter approached his table to congratulate him.

Harlan looked at him and said, "Hey, juvenile, you look sad."

He said, "I'm going through a pretty bad divorce."

Harlan said, "Is that all? Sit down. I've mastered that. What do you want, a smooth life or some great inspiration to write about? Some of my best songs came to me while I was in the middle of one of my divorces. If you handle this right, you can make thousands off of your heartbreak and misery. Just remember to set it down to a beat they can dance to."

Ol' Harlan,
Music Row, Nashville, Tennessee, 1997

From time to time country music will sell enough records to put itself in a position of thinking it's a pop phenomenon. Usually, the aftermath of one of these trends is an identity crisis. That's when the big guns get called in to bring its life and credibility back. Max D. Barnes has done this for country music time and time again. He's the real deal; he writes with the heart of a truck driver. When the music has to be brought back down to the basics, Max D. says what needed to be said all along. And he can do it in a three-minute song.

In the summer of 1987, I was living through an identity crisis of my own. I was in the middle of a divorce, drinking, drugging, and trying to figure out how to stand on my own and play the kind of music that was in my heart. Nothing I did seemed to work. It was the loneliest time of my life. I felt like a stray dog, but Max D. and his wife, Patsy, always welcomed me into their home. I knew I had a bed and a cup of coffee there anytime I needed it.

Max D. drove a silver Lincoln Continental in those days. The ashtray was always full of cigarette butts, and the glove compartment was usually full of killer country songs that he'd written. One afternoon in a studio parking lot, I was walking off the frustration of yet another bad day at the microphone, when Max D. pulled up in his silver cloud and said, "Get in."

When I got in, I said, "Max, just what the hell is country music anyway? I don't know anymore."

He said, "Listen to this song I just wrote. It's called 'Chiseled in Stone.'"

You don't know about lonely   *you don't know about sadness*
or how long nights can be   *till you face life alone*
till you've lived through the story   *you don't know about lonely*
that's still living in me   *till it's chiseled in stone.*

When it ended, Max D. said, "Son, that's country music."

Way down deep in the heart and soul of the matter is where Merle Haggard comes from. He is the truth—a well-traveled liver of life, a rascal, a poet, a picker, and our best singer. He's a cat among cats in the land of seventh chords. There's a line that Kristofferson wrote in a song called "The Pilgrim: Chapter 33" that fits Haggard. "A walking contradiction, partly truth, partly fiction. A pilgrim and a preacher and a problem when he's stoned."

He's Woody Guthrie's seed. The common man trusted him enough with his heart to let Merle write about it. He sings their stories with the timbre of a lost train hauling the ghost of Jimmie Rodgers through the dust of some blue heaven.

He has my vote. He has my confidence. I pledge allegiance to the Hag of the United States of America.

Merle Haggard, *Hollywood, California, 1994*

Summitt Studios, *Dallas, Texas, 1997*

Ryman Auditorium, *Nashville, Tennessee, 1994*

Nashville, *Tennessee, 1994*

Nashville,
Tennessee, 1994

Hag, *Dallas, Texas, 1997*

If a picture is worth a thousand words, a song must be worth at least a million pictures. Sometimes when I write a song, it feels as if I've just shaken hands with God himself.

Songwriting is among the purest gifts. It's amazing how powerful words can be. A great song lives forever, and when the right words and the right music find each other, and they make their way into my heart, it's almost more than I can take. Roger Miller once told me, "More than anything, it's about the song. Songs are magic carpets; they're your ticket to anywhere."

In my opinion, all should bow in deference to the songs and their creators. For with songs, there is further evidence that God speaks. Without them, we have nothing to sing about.

Go out to the edge, take a left, look straight up, and you'll find a warrior named Steve Earle. Steve writes songs about the things people really feel, but don't have the guts to say. I respect Steve Earle for what he stands for and for what he believes in. Some of my friends have died along the way for standing up for what they believed in, and there was a peroid of time when I was afraid we were gonna lose Steve too. A big old monkey jumped on his back and stayed there for way too long. I thought he was a goner. The devil had him in the palm of his hand and showed no signs of letting go. Somehow, Steve found the strength to put the quick move on him. He got out of his grasp and found his way home.

I was never so glad to see anybody make it back. I felt like a brother had returned from the war. I tried to write him a letter, but I couldn't get the words right. I never could seem to get him on the phone, so I did the only thing left to do. . . . I wrote him a song.

Steve Earle *talking blues*

"Crying,"

"Waiting,"

"Hoping'"

MARTY'S TALKING BLUES TO STEVE EARLE

He's got a big ole heart
beating in his chest.
And even at his worst,
he was still the best.
He just reappeared with
a whole new sound.
Sure is good to have
Steve back around.

He spent a few years
in hell itself.
When he beat the devil,
he up and left.
I still believe he's a
jewel in God's crown.
Sure is good to have
Steve back around.

Exceedingly rare,
extraordinary bird,
certified aviator,
this poet of words
escaped unharmed
from the lost & found.
Sure is good to have
Steve back around.
Sure is good to have
Steve back around.
Sure is good to have
Steve back around.
back around,
back around,
back around.

Dolly Parton

is one of those nearly untouchable people. Up until recently our relationship was not much more than a collection of "how do you do's" that we'd collected over several years backstage at award shows. I always felt that, if given the chance to get to know one another, we'd get along great.

I finally got the chance in 1995 when Dolly, Merle Haggard, Dwight Yoakam,

Willie Nelson, and I were chosen to help induct our friend, Roger Miller, into the Country Music Hall of Fame.

Of course, Merle, Dwight, and I started talking about Dolly from the minute she hit the set. After we'd gotten past talking about how good her dress fit, Merle said, "Well, everybody's always been so busy talking about her boobs, they usually overlook what a beautiful smile she

has. And her eyes reflect what a pure heart she has. Most of the world doesn't even know how deep a woman she is."

Dwight said, "Look how beautiful she is. She has an incredible aura around her. She looks like an angel."

I said, "She is the perfect example of a woman who has been blessed with it all. She can do anything she sets her mind to, and she gets it done her way, because she's smart. And if that doesn't work, she can kill you with that goddess charm she possesses. She's hard to say no to."

Willie, who'd been quiet the whole time, finally spoke up and said, "Do you think she has any rolling papers?"

We lost it. Rehearsal fell apart. When we told her what Willie had said, she lost it too. She has a wicked sense of humor.

After we'd taken care of immortalizing old Roger, I told Dolly how much I'd enjoyed working with her and I asked if we could get together some day to write a song. Soon after, she called and invited me to her office, "The Hooter House." I'm really proud of the songs we wrote, but I'm even more proud of having finally made friends with the coolest mountain girl in the world.

Dolly *at the Hooter House, 1998*

Wealth won't save your soul

I

As We journey along on lifes Wicked Road

so selfish ... ed.

you can tre ... silver and

gold.

Butt my fri ... poor Wicke

soul.

Hank Williams' *words and shirt, Nashville, Tennessee, 1996*

for when go ... s on high

To your ... y goodby

then its u ... yed from

the gold.

for my frie ... wicked

soul.

When the w ... ent day

for all of our wrongs then we ~~must~~ must pay

~~for~~ but the debt cant be paid with silver nor

gold.

no friends it won't save your poor wicked soul

II

The rich man like all will be gudged at that Time

but all of his wealth will be left behind

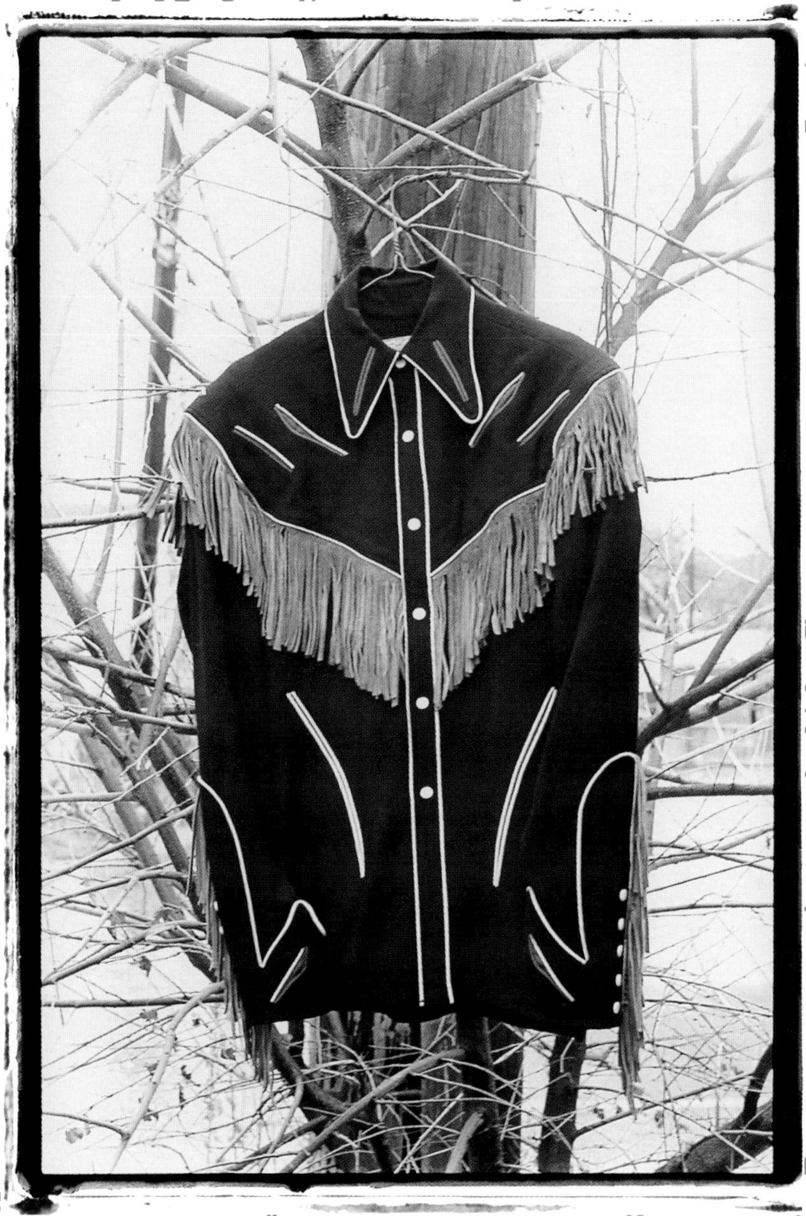

Hank Williams' *boots, Nashville, Tennessee, 1995*

"**Yeah,** I know what they say about Elvis Presley, but there's more than one King around here."

—*Roy Acuff fan, January 1995*

Del McCoury and Everett Lilly

Marty Stuart's back porch,
June 1, 1997

Marty Stuart
Interviews the Great Leroy Troy

Marty: What's the difference between bad moonshine and good moonshine?

Leroy: Bad moonshine is the kind that makes you real sick and gives you the headache. Good moonshine is the kind that when you swaller it, you don't make a face.

Marty: Have you ever seen an alien?

Leroy: No. But now Cordell Kemp, who lives up there at Defeated Creek—he's the feller that I picked up playing the banjer from—he's talked about seeing little people in the woods. But I don't know about that stuff. I probably wouldn't know one if I seen it. I believe in Big Foot, though.

Marty: Do you drive a car or a truck?

Leroy: A truck. A testimony to a good Chevy truck. It's a 1986 Silverado. It has over 300,000 miles on it. It might break down any day.

Marty: In your opinion is the Civil War over?

Leroy: No it is not. Reconstruction isn't over. Reconstruction is what we live with today.

Marty: What about the Confederate flag? We're not able to fly it anymore and be politically correct.

Leroy: I'm not able to not fly it. I do fly it. There's two sides to every story. The winner gets the spoils. I think every person has the right to celebrate their heritage and culture. There's good and bad in both. I ain't saying we was right about everything. We was wrong about some things. So was the Yanks.

Marty: What style do you call the music that you play?

Leroy: Hillbilly.

Marty: Hillbilly music sounds better to me on Saturday night, why do you think that is?

Leroy: Because it's the night of the Grand Ole Opry.

Marty: Do you have any thoughts on the 21st Century?

Leroy: Me and Daddy was talking about that the other day. We decided that we might ought to go out and buy three or four ricks of wood, and I might want to draw my money out of the bank.

Lester Flatt and Roy Acuff, *WSM Studios, 1974*

Fiddle
Men

Benny *Martin*

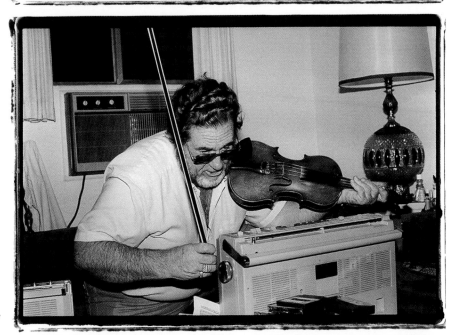

"**The Big** *Tige*"

John Hartford,
Goodlettsville,
Tennessee, 1996

Frasier Moss *and Mark O'Connor, Franklin, Tennessee, 1995*

Mr. "Uncle Josh" Graves, *"King of the Hound Dog Guitar,"*
Madison, Tennessee, 1997

The pride and joy of Flint Hill, North Carolina, Earl Scruggs is a pure American original who has helped define and revolutionize American music. He is a man of few words. Since he started recording in the 1940s, his banjo has done most of his talking. He has entertained the world since the day he hit town. His body of work is studied and taught by scholars. He's elevated the banjo from a comedic minstrel instrument to one of respect inside the world of music. What Satchmo is to New Orleans, what Miles Davis is to hip, what Sinatra is to Swing, that's what Earl Scruggs is to the banjo.

There's a pure magic about him. He is approached with reverence. If you were to stand him unannounced in the middle of Times Square playing his banjo, I'll guarantee that within fifteen minutes, the only sound you would hear would be the music he was playing.

Earl Scruggs, *Nashville, Tennessee, 1998*

Earl

Earl Scruggs and Mac Wiseman,
Coodlettsville, Tennessee

Mac

Doc

"Incident in A-Minor," *executed in three-quarter time, Roy Huskey Jr. and Doc Watson, Nashville, Tennessee, 1995*

Roy

Bill Monroe, Connie Smith, and Loretta Lynn,
Nashville, Tennessee, 1994

Big doings at Grandpa Jones' house (*Bashful Brother Oswald in the hot seat*),
Goodlettsville, Tennessee

Bashful Brother Oswald,
Coodlettsville, Tennessee

Dr. Ralph Stanley,
Nashville, Tennessee,
1997

The King of

Blue

Somewhere along the way, moonshine and dynamite collided. The result was a musical genius and a three-chord scholar named Jimmy Martin. He was baptized in the same fire that gave us Little Richard and Jerry Lee Lewis. He's part preacher, part prophet, and a card-carrying madman who is completely filled with the musical holy ghost. Time spent with the King of Bluegrass is not for the lily-livered or the faint of heart. It's more than a casual stroll through bongo land. One should expect a cosmic mountain ride through the kingdoms of music, coon hunting, love, heartbreak, liquor, dead batteries, more liquor, bright lights, dark valleys, two-toned shoes, heaven, hell, terror, tone, and timing. It's all in the neighborhood of B-natural. It's a place where everybody has 20/20 vision, but they're walking around blind.

Jimmy
Martin

grass

"Dance Hall Doctor," *Buck Owens, Bakersfield, California, 1997*

Buck Owens, *holding Don Rich's guitar, Bakersfield, California, 1997*

Little Jimmie Dickens, *Nashville, Tennessee, 1996*

Merle Travis

was a genius. He was a guitar great, prolific song-writer, journalist, teller of tall tales, actor, cartoonist, watch repairman, inventor, jack of all trades, and one of country music's pioneer statesmen.

I hung out with him for a weekend in the summer of 1981. We were in Mountain View, Arkansas, to judge the Annual Merle Travis Thumbpicking Contest. Guitar players who imitated Merle's style had come from all over the world to compete for the prize and to be in the presence of Travis himself.

We decided before we'd heard any of the contestants that regardless of how good or bad they were, we were going to declare all of them the first place winner. Merle's theory was that anybody who survived the winding mountain drive to where the contest was held should win for just making it up the hill. And we both thought that the main judge should be the bad guy to the ones who didn't place, not us.

Outside of the contest, it was mainly a weekend of roaring, playing music, telling stories, and playing cards. On Saturday night after the guitar show had ended and the true winner was finally determined, Travis and me struck up a serious poker game back at the hotel. After a couple of hours, I had played down to my last ten dollars. I had what I thought was a winning hand with three kings. He edged me with three aces. When I lost my ten dollars, he said, "Well, let's yak a while. I hear you're thinking about leaving J. R.'s band to go out on your own to be a country music singing star." I told him that I was.

He said, "Do you sing better than you play cards? If you're really going to do it, you're gonna be in for plenty of ups and downs. When the bad times come, that's when you'll see what you're made of on the inside. Hard times will come, and they usually get around to passing, if you don't pass out first."

With that, he poured himself another shot of booze, then pointed to his glass and said, "Sometimes bad luck has a way of following a feller around his whole life. If you ever go through a streak of this kind of sour luck and you finally find the strength to fight back, you'll need a little inspiration to get you back on track." He held up my ten dollar bill and said, "I'll sell you ten dollars worth of advice. What you do is:

1. Go buy yourself a new Cadillac.
2. Go to Nudie's and get some new cowboy clothes.
3. Find you a beautiful girl.
4. Find your guitar, dream up a new song, and start singing it.

Then watch the future start brightening up. Sometimes you just have to start brightening it up one little day at a time. What I'm trying to tell you is to never let show business break your heart. It ain't worth it. But regardless of all of that, always give them a good show."

He was the best at it. He was from the old line of hillbilly royalty. They knew how to shine on the out-

Twelve O'clock High, *Mountain View, Arkansas, 1981*

side even when they were crying on the inside. He had the act mastered.

Not long afterwards, I saw him for the last time. He was at a stoplight at the intersection of Gallatin Road and Due West in Madison, Tennessee. He was riding in a canary yellow Cadillac convertible. The license plates bore the name of his most popular song, "16 Tons." His new wife, Dorothy, was chauffeuring him about. The aviator sunglasses and his turquoise bolo tie were the perfect accessories to complement his forest green suit that Nudie had made for him and fully embroidered with deer and acorns all over it. He was a vision.

While we were waiting for the light to change, I said, "Hey Trav, how're you doing?"

He lowered his shades and winked. That told me all I needed to know.

When he pulled away, the sun caught the reflection of the rhinestones on his suit. It looked like a million crystals had shattered into a mirror and were bouncing back up into heaven. As he faded out of sight, I started thinking about the words to one of his songs:

I am a pilgrim and a stranger, traveling through this wearisome land. I've got a home in that yonder city, good Lord, and it's not, not made by hand.

Merle Travis, *Mountain View, Arkansas, 1981*

Wounded Knee, *South Dakota, 1994*

The Native American world is not exactly the kind of place you can casually drive up to, honk your horn, and start taking pictures. I respect their traditions and their culture too much to do that. My heart has always been led to honor them.

A friend of mine named John L. Smith has been going in and out of the Pine Ridge Reservation in South Dakota since 1963. To me, he's earned the ultimate form of accep-

tance that can be offered to a white man by the Indians—their trust. John L. is a highly regarded friend to the Lakota people. He's often called to be their voice and link to the outside world.

Knowing there's a responsibility that comes with going inside that world, I searched my heart to make sure my motives were pure, then asked John L. if he would take me along with him on one of his Pine Ridge journeys.

He took me, and thanks to him, the Lakota people welcomed me and made me feel like family.

The first person he introduced me to was William Horn Cloud. Mr. Horn Cloud was a direct descendent of a survivor of Wounded Knee. That was the first place he took me. He showed me point by point where his relatives were massacred by the U.S. Cavalry. They were buried in mass graves on Wounded Knee Hill. I wasn't ready for the feeling that overtook me when Mr. Horn Cloud began to pray and sing at the monument.

Along with being a historian and tour guide, Bill Horn Cloud was a pipemaker, world traveler, lecturer, and a builder of windmills. But what he was best known for inside the reservation was his singing. He was the leading singer for all of the nativistic religious meetings on Pine Ridge. He also served as head singer for the annual Sun Dance Ritual.

He told me that it was an honor to be able to sing. "Sometimes I sing for the people. Sometimes I sing for the four-legged creatures. Sometimes I sing for Wakan Tanka and the Great Mystery. Sometimes I sing for me. Today, I'm going to sing a song for you to take to Johnny Cash. If he likes it, tell him I need a horse."

I noticed several tape recorders in the house. When he finally found one that worked, he made up a song on the spot for me to take to Johnny Cash. Before we left his house, I took a walk around the yard and counted fourteen tired and broken down cassette recorders in the yard. His daughter, Laura Mae, told me they were his trophies. He told me, "My singing breaks those machines." I took them as status symbols for all that passed by. This was the home of the most important recording singer in Pine Ridge, South Dakota.

I took lots of pictures and notes that afternoon. I wrote in my journal, "Today, I spent the day with the most honorable man I believe I've ever met."

Mr. *Horn Cloud*

A song *for Johnny Cash*

Mr. Horn Cloud *and John L. Smith*

After the Sun Dance, *Badlands, South Dakota, fall 1994*

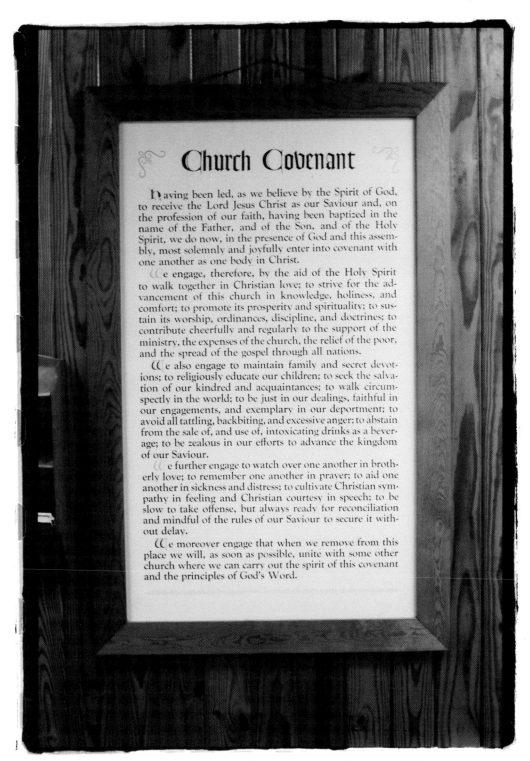

Church Covenant

Having been led, as we believe by the Spirit of God, to receive the Lord Jesus Christ as our Saviour and, on the profession of our faith, having been baptized in the name of the Father, and of the Son, and of the Holy Spirit, we do now, in the presence of God and this assembly, most solemnly and joyfully enter into covenant with one another as one body in Christ.

We engage, therefore, by the aid of the Holy Spirit to walk together in Christian love; to strive for the advancement of this church in knowledge, holiness, and comfort; to promote its prosperity and spirituality; to sustain its worship, ordinances, discipline, and doctrines; to contribute cheerfully and regularly to the support of the ministry, the expenses of the church, the relief of the poor, and the spread of the gospel through all nations.

We also engage to maintain family and secret devotions; to religiously educate our children; to seek the salvation of our kindred and acquaintances; to walk circumspectly in the world; to be just in our dealings, faithful in our engagements, and exemplary in our deportment; to avoid all tattling, backbiting, and excessive anger; to abstain from the sale of, and use of, intoxicating drinks as a beverage; to be zealous in our efforts to advance the kingdom of our Saviour.

We further engage to watch over one another in brotherly love; to remember one another in prayer; to aid one another in sickness and distress; to cultivate Christian sympathy in feeling and Christian courtesy in speech; to be slow to take offense, but always ready for reconciliation and mindful of the rules of our Saviour to secure it without delay.

We moreover engage that when we remove from this place we will, as soon as possible, unite with some other church where we can carry out the spirit of this covenant and the principles of God's Word.

Old Pearl Valley *Baptist Church, Arlington, Mississippi, 1999*

Old Nashville Highway, *Smyrna, Tennesseee*

"Nearer My God to Thee," *Dublin street musicians, 1994*

Chapel *in Santa Fe, New Mexico, 1996*

What we see now is like a dim image in a mirror; then we shall see face-to-face. What I know now is only partial; then it will be complete—as complete as God's knowledge of me.

1 Corinthians 13:12

"The Knoxville Girls," *fans at Dollywood, 1995*

The Fans

The first weekend I rode along as a guest of Lester Flatt, he played at a bluegrass festival in Glasgow, Delaware. He called for me to come sit by him in the front of the bus. He pointed out an older couple walking toward us. The lady was bringing a pie.

He said, "Do you see those people? They've been coming out to see me since 1945 when I was in Bill Monroe's band. When me and Earl left Bill to form our own outfit, they followed us. When Earl and me broke up, they stuck with me through that too. All it takes to

"America, what's it gonna take?"
Sunset Park, Pennsylvania, 1996

"Who caught who?"
St. Clairsville, Ohio, 1996

Good *People*

Sunset Park, Pennsylvania, 1996

Local *Outlaw*

keep folks like that coming back year after year is to treat them good. Always take the time with them for a picture, a handshake, and an autograph. Never forget them, and don't ever get above them, and they'll always be there for you."

That was the first piece of advice he ever gave me.

Once they've adopted you, country music fans are the kind of people that will cheer you on through the first days of slugging it out in the honky tonks. When the first hit finally comes, they're there. When you're red hot, white hot, going through the roof, or having your name become a household word, they'll stay right with you if you've kept up with them. When you're dragged through the mud for your failures and your weaknesses, they understand. As a rule, they're not judgmental people. They will pick you up out of the ashes and encourage you to come back again.

I guess the greatest piece of wisdom concerning fans was handed to Minnie Pearl by the Grand Ole Opry's founder, George D. Hay, the "Solemn Old Judge." Minutes before Minnie's first appearance on the Opry, he saw how scared she was and asked, "Honey, are you afraid?"

She said, "Yes sir, I am."

He said, "Here's what you do. You just go out there and love them, and they will love you right back."

Tattooed fans *in Salem, Ohio, 1996*

"One call gets 'em all," Division Street, Nashville, Tennessee, 1998

Mandy Barnett, *Nashville, Tennesee*

Angel from Montgomery

Bonnie Raitt,
Anaheim,
California, 1997

"Queenie" in Milan, Italy, 1994

Emmy and Rose, *Nashville, Tennessee, early 1980s*

Emmylou, *Nashville, Tennessee, early 1980s*

Pam Tillis, "The Coolest Cowgirl on Planet Earth," Nashville, Tennessee, 1998

"Blue Kentucky Girl," *Loretta Lynn, Nashville, Tennessee, 1995*

Shelby Lynne, *Nashville, Tennessee, 1997*

Bradley Barn

"**The King of** *Broken Hearts*"

I love people that are pure in what they do. George Jones is the purest country singer in the world. Just the sound of his voice can break your heart. On a cold winter week in 1994, MCA staged a recording event at Owen Bradley's studio in Mt. Juliet, Tennessee. The result was a record called the Bradley Barn Sessions. It was all about honoring George Jones. During the course of the week, Waylon Jennings, Jessi Colter, Mark Knopfler, Vince Gill, Ricky Skaggs, Trisha Yearwood, Connie Smith, Mark Chesnutt, Dolly Parton, Emmylou Harris, Alan Jackson, Tammy Wynette, Keith Richards, Leon Russell, and I all passed by the microphone to sing a song with George.

Sessions

"Golden Ring"

The most powerful moment was when George and Tammy sang together. Nobody knew what to expect before she arrived. The two hadn't recorded together since their divorce years earlier. When we first began to work on the song, everybody in the room seemed a little tense. But as music can sometimes do, it acted as an arbitrator and healer. By the end of the first chorus of "Golden Ring," we all knew that we were in the middle of three minutes of magic. She brought the best out in George. He did the same for her. For a moment, time stood still.

The funniest scene that week was watching George and Keith Richards. At first, George couldn't quite get a handle on Keith. Keith showed up with a jug of vodka to help him make it through the flight. From the minute he hit town he was very verbal that he was there to record with one of his all-time idols. To help prove it, he kept most of the guests of the Vanderbilt Plaza Hotel awake all night by blasting George Jones music from his speakers. He called it his pep rally. Said he had to get in shape to go work out with the man.

Before he and George actually met, Keith was in the lounge of the studio getting wound up to face him. George was in the studio, chain-smoking, wondering what he was going to do with Keith.

George called me over and said, "What's that boy's name that's fixin' to come in here?"

"Where Grass Won't Grow"

Dolly, George, and Emmy, *"Masters of Emotion"*

I said, "Keith Richards."

He said, "What's the name of that bunch he's with?"

I said, "The Rolling Stones."

He said, "Are they hot?"

I said, "Pretty damn hot!"

When Keith finally came in, I was touched by the amount of reverence and respect he showed George.

Keith said, "Man, I love you and I'm glad to be here."

George said, "We thank you."

He took out a cigarette and before he could even think about lighting it, Keith quick-drew his lighter and lit it for him. That's all it took to break the ice.

"The Love Bug"

George Jones *and Vince Gill*

Alan Jackson *and George Jones*

George asked Keith what he wanted to sing.
Keith said, "Burn Your Playhouse Down."

George said, "Boy, what made you think of that
one? That's one of the first songs I ever recorded."

Keith said, "I know. That's when I bought it."

It impressed me that the wildcard rocker in the
crowd brought the most obscure George Jones
song to the sessions.

When Keith left, I asked George what he
thought of him.

He said, "He's a good old boy. I like him. He's
kind of comical, like a cartoon. He reminds me of
Woody Woodpecker."

"A Good Year

"White Lightnin'"

"The *Possum*"

for the Roses"

Travis Tritt and I wound up in Keith's hotel room that night after the sessions. Keith played us rough mixes of the Stones' upcoming record, *Voodoo Lounge*. When I was saying my good-byes, Keith said, "Man, we did good today. We made Possum music."

"Burn Your Playhouse Down"

Keith and George

Travis

A buddy of mine named Ronnie Scaife and I wrote a song called "The Whiskey Ain't Workin' Anymore." When we finished it, we both thought it was a natural for Hank Williams Jr. We pitched it to him but he passed on it. A few days later I was in my car at the drive-thru window at a Burger King in Birmingham, Alabama, when a song called "Country Club" came on the radio. I didn't have a clue who was singing it, but I knew he was a singing fool. When the song ended, the disk jockey said it was a new artist named Travis Tritt. I thought this might be the guy for that whiskey song.

Not long after, I tuned into the *Tonight Show* where Travis was a guest. After he

sang, he took his guitar and crossed over to the panel to talk with Johnny Carson. Somehow, the conversation led to Travis picking up his guitar and singing Carson a song. Travis said, "Here's one I just wrote that I think you can relate to. It's called, 'Here's a Quarter, Call Someone Who Cares.'" He sang the fire out of it and cracked Carson up. That's when I knew he was a star. The next day I made a call to my publishing company and asked them to send a copy of "The Whiskey Ain't Workin' Anymore" to Travis Tritt.

He heard it, liked it, and recorded it. His producer, Gregg Brown, called me and asked if I'd come by the studio and play guitar on the record. I did. When I finished my

He snores better *than most people sing, Travis Tritt,*
Key West, Florida, 1996

part and was about to walk out the door, Gregg said, "How would you feel about singing the second verse?"

I said, "I don't think so. It doesn't need to be a duet. Travis said all that needed to be said."

Gregg said, "Try it. If you don't like it, we don't have to use it." I agreed and his idea worked. The song went on to become a number one record. Travis and I won a Grammy, an ACM Award, a CMA Award, and various other accolades. We teamed up for a tour called the "No Hats Tour" that sold lots of tickets, T-shirts, and pictures of us. After that, we had another hit and more awards came. Success seemed to follow us around. I'm proud of all of that, but what

means more to me than any of those things is the agreement the two of us made in my bus after we'd finished filming the video for "The Whiskey Ain't Workin' Anymore."

We made a bond that when we're old, ugly, fat, and bald, we'd still be there for one another. We became brothers that day and we've lived up to it ever since. We also put a clause in that bond called "the fun factor." It's simple: if it ain't fun, we don't do it. We've lived up to that too. I love him with all my heart. If he has any flaws, they're invisible to me. He's my closest friend. We've laughed our way through the thick and thin of most everything that's come our way since the day we met. Regardless of what the future holds, I don't see that ever changing.

Connie *with her dove guitar in Norway*

Connie Smith, *Jeannie C. Riley, and Skeeter Davis,*
Nashville, Tennessee, early 1980s

"**S**he sings and the sound of her voice is so sweet the birds hush their singing"

Queen of the

Kitty Wells, *Nashville, Tennessee, 1994*

Honky Tonk
Angels

Sister Sheryl Crow, *Nashville, Tennessee, 1995*

The Mississippi Mudcat & Sister Sheryl Crow

Oh Yeah, Oh Yeah, Oh Yeah. I am the main Mississippi Mudcat and always will be. Hello everybody. So there I was cruising through the country in my hotrod car—just visiting my friends up and down the backroads. I was driving slow—was driving slow and meditating on Sheryl Crow—on Sheryl Crow, folks. I'm telling you the truth. I'm telling you the truth. Yes I am.

Forty-three miles per hour, my gasoline was all gone. I was trying to look real cool, find my way back home. Dark, dark, dark. Driving slow—driving slow—just seemed like an endless supply of high-line poles and mailboxes. Then all of a sudden there stood by the mailbox at Route 4 Box 153 a damsel. Yes, a damsel in distress (alright). A damsel in 'dis dress, wearing high heels with big blue eyes that made the darkness crawl and a smile that could make a man cry. Yes I know. Yes I know. Somebody please ring that phone.

So I stopped and said, "Hello. You are without a doubt the most beautiful magnolia I have ever seen in my life. I love you." She said, "Shut up Marty Party. What are you doing tonight, riding around in that hotrod with that loud radio showing off them Chromium pipes and fold away wings?" I said, "I'm just looking for gas cans. Have you seen any?" (Ooo Wee, sometimes a fast rubber-tired shiny car is the thing to have.) She said, "Well Marty Party, do you want some company? You know my specialty is spotting gas cans." (Uh Oh.) Yeah, "Uh Oh," she said to me. She said to me, "What do you call this ride?" I said, "Baby just get in, get in, get in . . . I call this ride my rocketship."

"You don't know how it feels to be me"
—Tom Petty

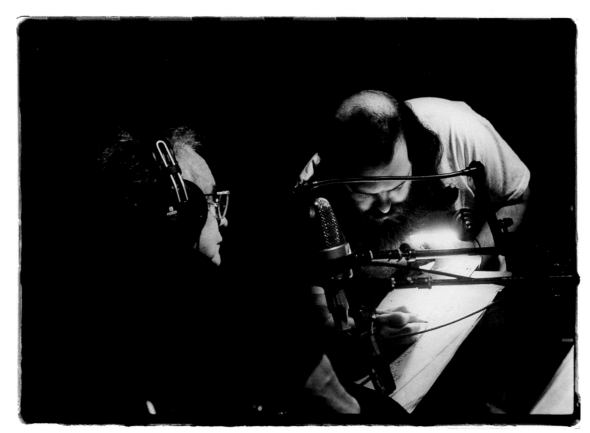

Johnny Cash, *Rick Rubin,*

The Unchained
Sessions, Los Angeles,
California, 1997

and Tom Petty

Beck-*a-doodle-boogie-woogie,*
Los Angeles, California, 1997

Elvis Costello, *January, 1998*

*Dwight
Yoakam*

Little Richard

"The Quasar of Rock and Roll,"
Nashville, Tennessee, 1994

Shel Silverstein, *Key West, Florida*

Boom

Boom

Boom

Boom

John Lee Hooker, *Anaheim, California*

B. B. King, *recording "Confessing the Blues," Hollywood, California, 1997*

Country Boys' Late Night Studio A—
Johnny Cash, Billy Sherrill, and Ray Charles, early 1980s

Brother Phillip Holloway, *Happy Hollow Holiness Church, 1989*

Jerry and *Tammy Sullivan*

Jerry Sullivan *in Ryman Auditorium*

During the first half of the twentieth century, some charismatic Christians on the backroads of the South held their worship services in settings called Brush Arbors. Brush Arbors were makeshift churches set up out in the country by placing rough hewn poles in the ground and covering them with the brush from trees. It provided shade from the sun and served as an umbrella for the people while they worshipped.

Jerry Sullivan fell in love with the Gospel as a young man and got saved during a Brush Arbor revival meeting in 1942. His brother, Arthur Sullivan, a Pentecostal preacher, encouraged Jerry and his nephews, Enoch and Emmett, to make their style of string band music into Gospel. As Brush Arbors grew into formal churches, the Sullivans contributed an original kind of music to the revolution of the United Pentecostal movement. It was high-spirited rhythm-based music driven by the mandolin and the fiddle, and it was sang in the lonesome tones of blue-grass and mountain music.

Today, those songs are remembered mostly by the remnants of a vanishing congregation of the Brush Arbors. Jerry Sullivan and his daughter, Tammy, are among the last of the traveling musicians still singing on the original backroads circuit. The Elders have selected Tammy as the keeper of the flame for that old Pentecostal style of singing because of the message that lives in her heart and the new holy fire that she possesses for carrying it to a new generation.

THE HAPPY

" **W**hen I was sixteen years old, I went to the altar at church and openly dedicated my life to the Lord. That's when I felt the call of the Gospel. It's been a great journey. There've been good times and many times of struggle. But when something comes my way that seemingly would make my life easier or richer, if it's not the Gospel, I can't do it, because I fell head over heels in love with Jesus at that altar and never got over it. The only thing I want to do is love him more. If he'll teach me how, I will."

—*Vestel Goodman*

GOODMANS

Sister Vestel and Brother Howard, *singing "Amazing Grace," July 8, 1999, Nashville, Tennessee*

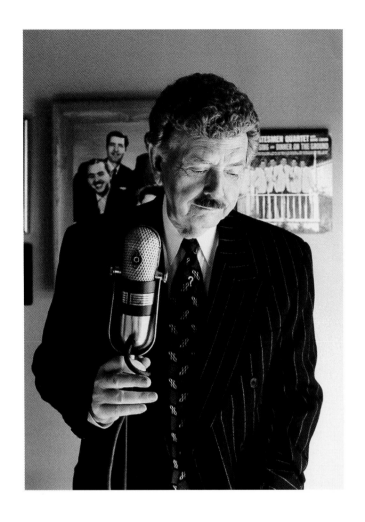

Jake Hess, *the best friend
a Gospel song ever had*

P ops Staple, without a doubt, is the finest in Jesus' name guitar player to ever come out of the Mississippi Delta. He can make a Fender Jazzmaster preach the Gospel. Son Thomas, a great blues guitar player from Leland, Mississippi, once said, "If you play the blues, you're working on the devil line. If you play the gospel, you're working on the God line." I asked Pops what he thought about that. He said, "I'm a Gospel man, but don't you know, when the good Lord looks down on this world, he gets a bad case of the blues."

The Staple Singers,
Los Angeles, California

"In the valley *he restoreth my soul"*

Dottie Rambo is the most gifted songwriter I've ever known. Her songs are a wide-open path that leads straight to her spirit. And looking into her spirit is like staring directly into the sun. It's almost more than the eye can bear. But there's something irresistible about it. Maybe it's the mystique that lies behind the veil of the unseen heaven-world she puts into words so well. Some of the lines in her songs tell her story.

"He looked beyond my
faults and saw my needs"
"Tears are a language
God understands"
"I'm a prisoner of love"

I'm humbled in her presence. I see God's fingerprints all over her work. She is a vessel whom God has used many times to represent Him, a modern day human being who has been granted divine permission to explore His holiest places. In turn, she composes words of encouragement, reminders, hope, insight, and the knowledge of a peaceful promised land that's so far away, yet so near.

The Thin Man

Porter Wagoner,
Nashville, Tennessee

Way back in the days of Mississippi and me
I saw him for the first time on an old Quasar TV
He came on like a storm, flashing lightning, fire and rain
He sparkled like a diamond
The thin man from West Plains

I felt it in his footsteps, I heard the clicking of his heels
He told stories about a way of life
That said exactly how I feel
He'd come in for a visit, then leave just like he came
Fade right into nowhere
The thin man from West Plains

He sang a song about a rich man who was all broke up inside
He sang a song about a careless love and the cold, hard facts of life
He talked about a country church that took the Lord in vain
Sad but true, felt like I knew
The thin man from West Plains

The first time I shook his hand, it was like I'd known him all my life
I wouldn't trade ten mercury dimes, and two old Barlow knives
For a friend like that comes once around
Words fail me to explain
How I feel these days about the good old days
And the thin man from West Plains

The years faded like the rhinestones on one of his old worn out suits
I went running wild, lost my style
Got down to what's the use
But when he'd see me coming, there was no need to explain
He'd draw me in like some old friend
The thin man from West Plains

I woke up in a valley, there was nothing in my soul
Somewhere, somehow along the way, I let the devil take control
Then I reached down in my heart, beyond all the hurt and shame
And found the words once said to me
By the thin man from West Plains

from West Plains

If Jesus came to your house to spend a day or two, if he came unexpected, I wonder what would you do?

When you saw him comin', would you meet him at the door, with your arms outstretched in welcome to your heavenly visitor?

Or would you need to change some things before you let him in, like burn some magazines and put the Bible where they'd been?

Could you let him walk right in, or would you rush about to hide your worldly things and put some hymn books out?

Oh, I know you'd give your nicest room to such an honored guest.

And all the food you'd serve him would be your very best.

And you'd keep assuring him that you were glad to

have him there, that serving him in your home was joy beyond compare.

But would your family conversation keep up its normal pace, and would you find it hard each meal to say a table grace?

Would you be glad to have him meet your very closest friends, or would you hope that they would stay away until his visit ends?

Would you take him with you everywhere you planned to go, or maybe change your plans for just a day or so?

Would you be glad to have him stay forever or on and on, or would you sigh with great relief when finally he had gone?

You know it might be interesting to know the things you'd do if Jesus came in person to spend some time with you.

Porter Wagoner

"Baby, *your grandpa was a man named Hank Williams." Hank Williams Jr. with his daughter, Katie, 1995*

bought a piece of old stained glass in Austin, Texas, in 1997. When I got it home and restored it, I uncovered these words etched into the background:

Then move the trees
the copses nod
wings, flutter, voices hover clear
oh just and faithful knight of God,
ride on the prize is near
so pass I hostel, hall and grange
by bridge and ford, by park and pale
all armed I ride, what'er betide
until I find the Holy Grail

Johnny Cash, *1999*

Montego Bay, Jamaica, 1999

I learned that these words were taken from Alfred Lord Tennyson's poem "Sir Galahad." I hung the piece in my basement and forgot about it. During the final days of working on my record, *The Pilgrim*, I was struggling to find the proper ending. The story is about a man's journey to hell and back as he tries to outrun true love. It's a powerful story that called for a heavy-handed piece of drama for the finale. I walked past this piece of glass one evening and Tennyson's words caught my eye. It struck me like a revelation that I'd finally found my ending. I immediately thought of J. R. His voice seemed perfect for the part. I called him and told him the story of *The Pilgrim* and read him the verse. He liked it and agreed to come by the studio to record it the following week.

I set up a full session but he forgot to show. I called for J. R. the next day but was told he'd gone to his home in Jamaica. I wrote him a letter, reminding him that he'd forgotten the session. He called me and said he'd do it as soon as he got back to Nashville. Weeks turned into months and he still hadn't surfaced, so I contacted him and asked if I brought the equipment to Jamaica, would he do it there. He said, "C'mon."

J. R.,
Cinnamon Hill, 1999

I had my sound engineer, Matt Spicher, gather the equipment we needed. We boarded a plane, and, in the spirit of Alan Lomax and Ralph Peer, we embarked on a field recording adventure, hoping to capture the sound of an American icon in his natural habitat. I knew it would be interesting. Other than recording some Bible verses on tape, J. R. hadn't said hello to a microphone in months.

We flew into Montego Bay expecting to spend one night. That one night turned into three of the nicest days of my life. We set up the recording gear in the Great Room at John and June's house. At five in the afternoon, he came downstairs, looking cool in his "Man in Black" persona, and gave "Sir Galahad" a flawless reading. The next couple of days we feasted, had heart-to-heart talks by the sea, swiped golf balls from the tourists at the golf course, visited graveyards, and picked flowers for June. On the last evening, J. R. gave his first informal concert in almost two years in the living room. The next day, I left Jamaica feeling good. Everything's all right with me as long as I know Johnny Cash is all right. And he is.

Swiping from the rich, *giving to the poor*

Bill Monroe

first heard Bill Monroe on an old 78 r.p.m record. The song was "Little Community Church." It cost me seventy-five cents. The first time I met Bill Monroe was in the summer of 1970. He performed a concert at the National Guard Armory in Jackson, Alabama. After the show, I bought one of his records, so I could get him to autograph it. While he was writing his name on the cover, I told him that I'd just gotten a mandolin and I wanted to learn to play it like him. When he hand-

ed me the album back, he reached into his pocket, pulled out his mandolin pick, and gave it to me. He told me to "go home and learn how to use it."

That night marked the beginning of a friendship that lasted a quarter of a century. From the earliest days when he let me carry his mandolin case from the bus to the dressing room to the last day when Ricky Skaggs, Vince Gill, Emmylou Harris, Connie Smith, Ralph Stanley, Patty Loveless, Roy Huskey Jr., Stuart Duncan, and I stood on stage at the Ryman

The *chicken reel*

Last Winter

and played him home. He was an endless source of inspiration to me. For twenty-five years I watched him, studied him, and loved him. I respected him because he never compromised his beliefs or his music in any way. He drove it with a sledge hammer to the bitter end.

A few months before his stroke, I spent an afternoon at his farm. We took pictures, reminisced, and played some music. He wasn't feeling good, but he dressed up, and gave me a full afternoon in front of the camera. It was to be his last photo session. I cherish that day.

At some point during that afternoon I asked him if he was happy with the way his life had turned out. Without hesitation, he said, "Yes sir. I've played for several presidents, and some of them gave me awards. I've played all around the world. I helped Elvis get his start with my song 'Blue Moon of Kentucky.' I love my country. I've been baptized in the River Jordan. I've got lots of friends, and there's

some powerful good people out there pulling for me, and bluegrass music is loved by people everywhere. Things turned out mighty fine."

I could tell he'd thought it over, and these were the main accomplishments by which he'd measured his life's work. He put eighty-something years into a few short words. That was just like him. He always communicated better when a lot of words weren't involved. For instance, in the early days of knowing him, I enjoyed the times he'd let me ride along with him on his bus. I'd ask him to teach me mandolin tunes. His way of teaching was to tell me the title and play it a time or two. Then he'd expect me to fall in and play it with him. His was the Old Indian style. Instead of talking about it, he taught by doing. If I couldn't get it right, he'd move on to another song. I hated it when I wasn't quick enough. I wanted to impress him. Sometimes, this would go on for hours. He had his ways of testing me to see how much I could take. He'd work me hard until it was

time to quit. I always tried to wait him out until he wanted to stop. I don't think he was ever the one to lay down the mandolin first.

As the sun started sinking that afternoon at his farm, I could sense that he was getting tired. He said, "So, you think we did all right?"

I told him I thought we got some great pictures. Then I put down my camera and picked up one of his mandolins. I handed him his old mandolin and asked if we could play "Lonesome Moonlight Waltz,"

one of my favorite songs by him. Something told me this would be the last time we'd be doing this. When the song ended, I hugged his neck and told him that I loved him.

He said, "You learned good, boy."

Bill Monroe *teaching Jacob's Ladder to Katie Conway*

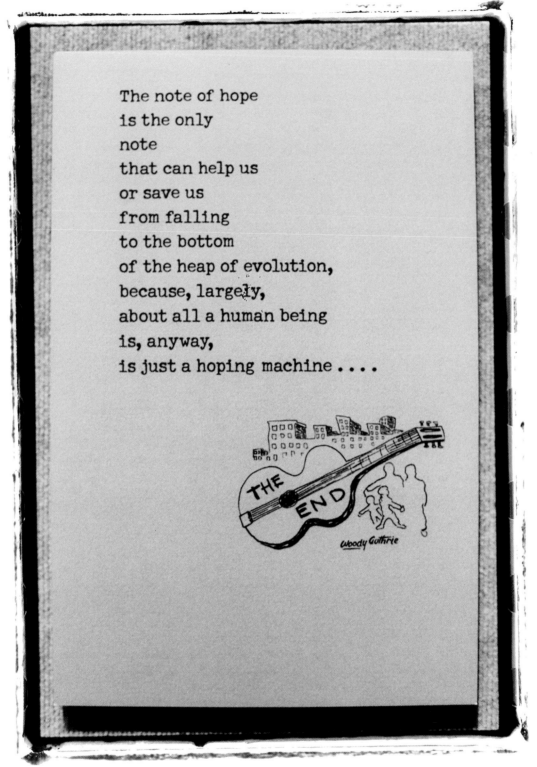

The note of hope
is the only
note
that can help us
or save us
from falling
to the bottom
of the heap of evolution,
because, largely,
about all a human being
is, anyway,
is just a hoping machine . . . .

THE
END
Woody Guthrie

"Woody Guthrie's words on Gene Autry's wall,"
Autry Museum of Western Heritage, 1999